Ahlul Bayt

The Holy Family of Prophet Muhammad (PBUH&F)

Written & Illustrated
by Alia Bazzi

Rev. date: 06/10/2014

To order additional copies of this book, contact:
Xlibris LLC
1-888-795-4274
www.Xlibris.com
Orders@Xlibris.com

Ahlul Bayt

The Holy Family of Prophet Muhammad (PBUH&F)

Written & Illustrated by
Alia Bazzi

Acknowledgments

Al-ḥamdu lillāh with all humbleness, Allah Almighty allowed me to fulfill my oath to Ahlul Bayt upon visiting one of the Holy Shrines.

A special note of thanks and acknowledgement to the following individuals:

My dear parents, Youssef and Hayat Bazzi for their continuous support and encouragement.

My brother, Ali Bazzi for whose motivation and persistence encouraged me to finish what I started.

My sister Fatimah Bazzi for her creative writing assistance.

My brothers Ahmad and Mohammad Bazzi for their constructive criticism on the artwork.

An additional special thanks and acknowledgement to the following individuals:

Sayed Dr. Riadh Ahmad, a prominent religious scholar in North America who resides in Montreal Canada, for his time to review the religious and historical content of the book.

My dear Aunt Souad Bazzi Habhab, an Educator who holds degrees in Philosophy and English Literature, for revising and editing the book.

بسم الله الرحمن الرحيم

إِنَّمَا يُرِيدُ اللَّهُ لِيُذْهِبَ عَنْكُمُ الرِّجْسَ أَهْلَ الْبَيْتِ وَيُطَهِّرَكُمْ تطهيرا

(سورة الأحزاب : آية 33)

"Verily, Allah has decreed to purify you, O' Ahlul Bayt, and sanctify you in a perfect way"

(Surah 33. Al-Ahzab, Ayah 33)

8

The introduction

The Holy Prophet said, "The similitude of my Ahlul Bayt is that of the Ark of Noah (Safinat Nouh), whoever embarks it, is saved and whoever turns away from it is perished". This book will shed the light on Ahl Al-kisa (People of the Cloak), Prophet Muhammad, Imam Ali, Syeda Fatima, Imam Al-Hassan and Imam Al-Hussein, who are the foundation of Ahlul Bayt. Ahlul Bayt (Members of the house of the Prophet), are the successors of Prophet Muhammed, who are divine individuals and teachers of the Islamic faith. They teach us how to follow the Holy Quran and obey Allah. As mentioned by our Holy Prophet Muhammed "Oh people I leave amongst you two things, which if you follow you never go astray. They are the book of Allah and my Ahlul Bayt".

The Holy Prophet Muhammad ibn Abdullah
(Peace be upon Him and His Family)

It was the darkest of times in the Arabian Peninsula, where the Holy Kaaba (House of Allah in Mecca) was occupied by nonbelievers who worshipped idols made of stone and wood. These idols could not speak, hear nor benefit man in any way. Injustice, violence and hate were widespread amongst Arab tribes. The strong killed the weak; the rich showed no mercy. Poverty, slavery and female infanticide was common amongst people.

Amidst these dark times of disbelief, a bright light from above spread across from sunset to sunrise marking the birth of the last and final prophet of Islam, the Holy Messenger of Allah. His name was "Muhammad" which translates as "Praiseworthy". Allah sent Prophet Muhammad, ibn (son of) Abdullah, as a mercy to mankind, to guide them from the path of darkness and idol worship to the path of light and salvation to the One True God (Allah).

"And we have not sent you, [O Muhammad], except as a mercy to the worlds." (21:107)

Prophet Muhammad was from the Banu Hashim tribe who were direct descendants of Prophet Abraham. Prophet Muhammad's Grandfather Abd Al-Muttalib was a prominent leader from Banu Hashim tribe and was known as a caretaker of the Holy Kaaba.

At age 40, Prophet Muhammad received his first revelation from Allah through angel Gabriel. He was to recite Arabic verses from the Holy Quran (Words of Allah). Angel Gabriel informed the Prophet that his mission was to restore the worship of The One True God "Allah" and "You" Muhammad are the final Messenger of Allah. The Quran was considered as the most important miracle of Prophet Muhammad to prove his prophethood to the nonbelievers.

Throughout his prophethood, Muhammad continued to receive a verse, chapter or a complete chapter of the Quran. Prophet Muhammad continuously proclaimed his message and mission that was entrusted to him by Allah. This was made possible by his strong faith and support of his wife Syeda Khadija, family and followers.

Slowly and gradually Islam was embraced by believers and nonbelievers alike.

Imam Ali Al-Murtada
(Peace be upon Him)

On Friday the 13th of the month of Rajab, Ali, ibn Abu Talib and first cousin of the Prophet Muhammad was born in the city of Mecca in the Holy Kabaa. Fatima bint (daughter of) Assad, the wife of Abu Talib, went to the Kaaba to pray during her pregnancy. As she was praying, the walls of the Kaaba broke open for her to enter and immediately closed behind her. Not long after, Fatima gave birth to her baby boy Ali.

For three days Fatima and her newly born were in the grace of God and his angels. God honored Imam Ali with greatness by allowing him to be the only person to have been born in His Holy House, the Kaaba.

Abu Talib, like most of the Meccans during that time, faced financial crises and needed assistance and care with his many children. The Holy Prophet took Imam Ali under his care and presence. Through the years a special relationship was created between Imam Ali and Prophet Muhammad. This relationship was witnessed on the holy day of Ghadir Khumm, in which the Holy Prophet performed a ceremony declaring Imam Ali as his successor, giving him the title 'Commander of the faithful' - *Amīr al-*Mu'minīn.

Imam Ali's life with the Holy Prophet was marked with great successes. Prophet Muhammad said to Imam Ali, "**You are to me like the rank of Harun to Musa, except that there will be no prophet after me.**" The Prophet repeated this on numerous occasions when referring to Imam Ali as his brother and closest companion.

Following in the footsteps of the Holy Prophet and the teachings of the Holy Quran, Imam Ali was a very benevolent (good) person. He cared deeply for the well-being of others, especially those in need, the poor and the orphans. Imam Ali was known as 'Abo Al-Aytam' (father of the orphans) because he felt his main concern was to help and guide the orphans.

Imam Ali was known for his physical strength, courage, wisdom and most importantly his unconditional faith in Allah; his courage helped lead victorious battles alongside the Holy Prophet against the nonbelievers.

فاطمة

Syeda Fatima Al-Zahraa
(Peace be upon Her)

The Prophet's descendants all trace back to his daughter Syeda Fatima Al-Zahraa, from his wife Khadijah. Allah bestowed upon Syeda Fatima the title 'Syedatun Nisa Al-Alamin' which means "Leader of all the women of the world".

The Holy Prophet gave his daughter the highest respect and always showered her with love and kindness. He also said:

"Whoever hurts Fatima, hurts me, and whoever hurts me, hurts Allah, exalted be His Majesty!"

As the years went by, Imam Ali married Prophet Muhammad's daughter, Syeda Fatima Al Zahraa and raised a family. Like her husband, Imam Ali, Syeda Fatima stood alongside her father, throughout all his difficulties. Her role in Islamic history was critical because she helped educate women and more importantly, she helped educate them about the religion of Islam.

Together Imam Ali and Syeda Fatima raised an exemplary loving Muslim family. Prophet Muhammad loved his grandsons Imam Al-Hassan and Imam Al-Hussein dearly.

Imam Al-Hassan Al-Mujtaba
(Peace be upon Him)

On the 15th of the month of Ramadan in the city of Medina, the first grandchild was born in the household of our Prophet. The Prophet was very happy to see his grandson. He held him and embraced him close to his heart and recited the Azan (Islamic call to prayer) in his right ear and then recited the Eqamah in his left ear (Similar to Islamic call to prayer). Not long after, Angel Gabriel visited our beloved Prophet congratulating him and informing him that Allah had chosen the name Al-Hassan for the newly born. At that time, Al-Hassan was a new and unique name which means good or goodness *(Which is derived from the divine goodness of Allah).*

At multiple occasions our beloved Prophet Muhammad said, "Al-Hassan and Al-Hussein are the masters of youth in heaven and that they are Imams whether they decided to stand (fight) or sit (make peace)".

Imam Al-Hassan was brought up taking in his most pivotal role as a missionary of Islam with his family. He was most like his grandfather both in his physical appearance and great manners. After the Prophet died, people would look at Imam Al-Hassan to remember him.

Imam Al-Hassan learned from his grandfather that the best way to enter the hearts and minds of people was to treat them with tolerance, kindness and respect. Imam Al-Hassan was also very brave in facing challenges. He helped and fought alongside his father, Imam Ali, on the battlefields against the nonbelievers and enemies.

Upon his father's death, Imam Al-Hassan briefly succeeded as the righteous caliph before entering in a peace treaty agreement with Umayyad ruler, Muawiyah ibn Abi Sufyan. Muawiyah had assumed the caliphate and disregarded the pledge of allegiance given from the people of Kufa and Mecca to Imam Al-Hassan. To scatter the unity and love the people had for Imam Al-Hassan, Muawiyah bribed and threatened the people until they were no longer united to stand against him. It was important at the time for Imam Al-Hassan to enter this peace treaty agreement. Having the supreme Islamic interest in mind, Imam Al-Hassan stepped aside to protect the unity and stability amongst all the Muslims.

Imam Abu Abdullah Al-Hussein
(Peace be upon Him)

Tears streamed down the Prophets face, upon the birth of Imam Al-Hussein. His birth was marked as a very sad moment for the Holy Prophet because the Angel Gabriel informed the Prophet of Imam Al-Hussein's tragic martyrdom in the battle of Karbala. The Prophet's love and affection towards Imam Al-Hussein was witnessed on a daily basis. Prophet Muhammad told his followers, "Al-Hussein is from me and I am from Al-Hussein".

After the death of the three most important men in Islam; Prophet Muhammad, Imam Ali and Imam Al-Hassan, Imam Al-Hussein was left alone to fight the corruption that was taking over Islam by Yazid ibn Muawiyah. Yazid succeeded his father to the throne. He demanded from Imam Al-Hussein to give oath of allegiance to him from Medina. The Imam replied back saying, "A person like me would not give the oath of allegiance to a person like Yazid who has violated all tenets of Islam". Not long after, the people of Kufa wrote to Imam Al-Hussein asking for his help and protection from the evil doings of Yazid. Upon receiving the letters pleading for help, Imam Al-Hussein headed towards Kufa along with his family and close friends. But before they reached the city of Kufa, Yazid's army was waiting for Imam Al-Hussein and his followers in Karbala where the battle took place. Imam Al-Hussein, with his 72 male warriors, was up against thousands of Yazid's men.

On the tenth day of Muharam, after all his warriors were killed, Imam Al-Hussein was outnumbered and left alone surrounded by all his enemies. The Heaven's angels mourned as the sky turned red on the martyrdom of Imam Al-Hussein.

The martyr of the third successor of the Holy Prophet was marked as the turning point in Islam. Imam Al-Hussein is remembered every year during the ten mourning days of Ashura. His martyrdom symbolizes the awakening call against all oppression and evil doings.

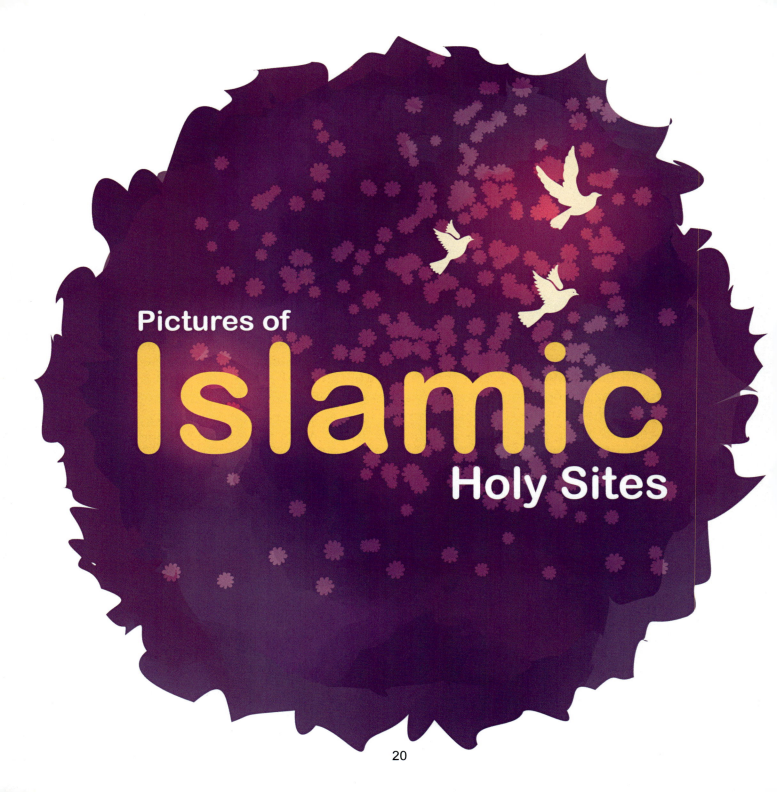

Pictures of
Islamic
Holy Sites

The Holy Kaaba is located in the city of Mecca, Saudi Arabia.

Al-Masjid An-Nabawi is located in the city of Medina, Saudi Arabia.

The Shrine of Imam Ali is located in the city of Najaf, Iraq.

The grave of Imam Al-Hassan is located in Jannatul Baqi in the city of Medina, Saudi Arabia

The Shrine of Imam Al-Hussein is located in the city of Karbala, Iraq.

25

Printed in the United States
By Bookmasters